BEACH NUTS

SIMON DREW'S BOOK OF LUDICROUS LIMERICKS

The limerick writer should strive
to ensure that his verse comes alive.
It's a bit of a bore
to say: 'this is line 4,'
and it's worse to say: 'this is line 5.'

Antique Collectors' Club

to Caroline
and to Buzz

There once was a mouse in Manhattan
whose bottom displayed a strange pattern.
The chair said Wet Paint
and he thought 'No it aint,'
so that was the thing that he sat on.

©2009 Simon Drew
World copyright reserved

ISBN 978-1-90537-736-7

British Library Cataloguing-in-Publication Data
A catalogue record for this book is available from the British Library

Printed in China for the Antique Collectors' Club Ltd., Woodbridge, Suffolk

Oliver Cromwell had found
a halo thrown out on the ground,
and as you can tell
it fitted him well;
you can see that his head is so round.

Isambard Kingdom Brunel
was not feeling terribly well
so with death on his mind
he quickly designed
a bridge linking heaven with hell.

He painted gold cornfields in June
and crows by the light of the moon
    and portraits that glow,
      but not many know –
Van Gogh had an ear for a tune.

A wedding guest known just as Drake
was seen to escape on a lake.
        And after a pause
            they found out the cause:
it seems he had eaten the cake.

A bride wears a dress with a train;
it's made of pure white with no stain.
And when she's said 'Yes'
she can take off that dress
and bask in a bath of champagne.

MOVING HOUSE

Bert had a change of address:
the move had been nothing but stress.
But the house is sublime
and, given some time,
it'll seem a bit less of a mess.

"Why does your grin seem so wide?"
And the old water spaniel replied:
   "Like the lion that roars
      to gleeful applause,
I'm trying to show off my pride."

King Harold was feeling the strain:
"The Hastings Gazette is insane.
    They want me to sit
      by a tapestry kit.
It's the damned paparazzi again."

Bridge is a very strange game:
approach it without any shame.
    If you play the wrong card
    say: "life is so hard,"
and your partner should take all the blame.

Queen Victoria visits the Great Exhibition:

The Queen, whilst observing a hutch,
said: 'Rabbits look soft to the touch.'
    So they gave her a feel
    and she whispered: 'Big deal!
I suppose we're amused, but not much.'

Leonardo da Vinci loved tea:
he said that it helped him to see.
   "I needed a cuppa
      to paint the last supper
and monks gave me biscuits for free."

A german named Gunter would spend
many hours to explain to a friend –
    his feelings were strong
    that his grammar was wrong
and a sentence should with a verb end.

When a doctor is doing his rounds
he may prefer hunting with hounds
    or he might get a call
    from a little white ball
when the golf course is so out of bounds.

When Raleigh brought fags back to Britain
the Queen was immediately smitten.
"Tobacco's so cool,"
she slurred through her drool.
"so now there's no need to smoke kitten".

Cholesterol works like a rat:
it's the key hidden under the mat.
 Doctors are pests
  insisting on tests
and it turns out, the truth is I'm fat.

Doctor Findlay will see to your ills
by giving you little white pills
    but once in a while
    he'll dress up in style
in a skirt made of tartan (with frills).

The Queen, having nothing to do,
went down to the river at Kew.
"The swans look divine
    (I'll remind you – they're mine)
and they do make spectacular stew."

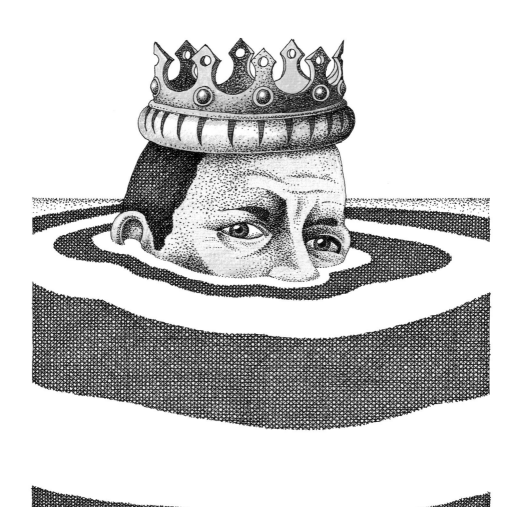

It never occurred to Conute
he shouldn't have worn his best suit.
It seemed such a bore
but just to be sure
he did wear one wellington boot.

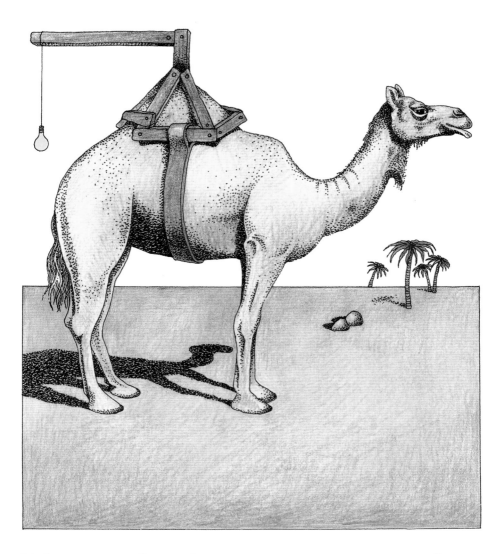

When putting the name to a mammal
try testing its dental enamel
    but if you're still stumped
    and find that it's humped
there'll be light at the end of the camel.

The cow that jumped over the moon
had flown there beneath a balloon.
She said as she ran:
"It's a small step for man
but a leap for a jersey called June."

A tooth fairy said: 'It seems odd:
no matter wherever I've trod,
   most people feel
    a fairy's not real.
In fact we're as solid as God.'

When Friday met Robinson Crusoe
in a jungle that could be by Rousseau
he said without malice:
'I'll build you a palace
though it may take me ages to do so.'

When Robinson Crusoe met Friday
he said: 'This is looking like MY day.
　　You miserable wretch
　　　I want you to fetch
a steak with some chips on the side, eh!'

Charles Darwin recalled an election:
"While voting, I chose, on reflection,
a man with a cape
who resembled an ape.
I call it my natural selection."

Edward (whose surname is Lear)
can hardly restrain the first tear:
   the pussycat bride
   has suddenly died
and the owl has announced that he's queer.

The hippo's a creature of taste:
it's fond of a fine bloater paste.
But then it may take
a small chocolate cake
though none of it's good for the waist.

The despicable crimes of Rasputin
would never require much disputin:
    he couldn't resist
     a stab and a twist
then, when they were down, put the butin.

There once was a soldier called Caesar
who fancied a pizza from Pisa.
   However, his home
    was way off in Rome,
so he went and found one in the freezer.

The scene is a chamber with beds
with Anne Boleyn sewing gold threads.
    With a hand at her throat
    she tossed up a groat
and Henry, her husband, cried: 'Heads'.

A young girl who came from Caerphilly
declared that she wasn't so chilly
so tore off her clothes
in a pub called the Rose
attracting young men, willy nilly.

ayer's

There once was a sailor called Cook
(I've seen his exploits in a book):
    "I name this Australia,
        and although it's a failure,
it might do to house the odd crook."

A pig in a barrel of glue,
was bored and had nothing to do;
so he whiled away hours
by pressing wild flowers
(by the end of the day he'd pressed two).

A mischievous cat from Bengal
found a fat smiling head on a wall;
   with egg on his face
   he suffered disgrace
when he caused it to have a great fall.

In Stratford on Avon one day
a bloke with a quill wrote a play:
   he wrote round the clock
    despite writer's block
for where there's a Will there's a way.

At the zoo, william shakespeare would stare
at the beasts that they had in their care.
    But looking for more
    he opened a door . . . .
so, exit pursued by a bear.

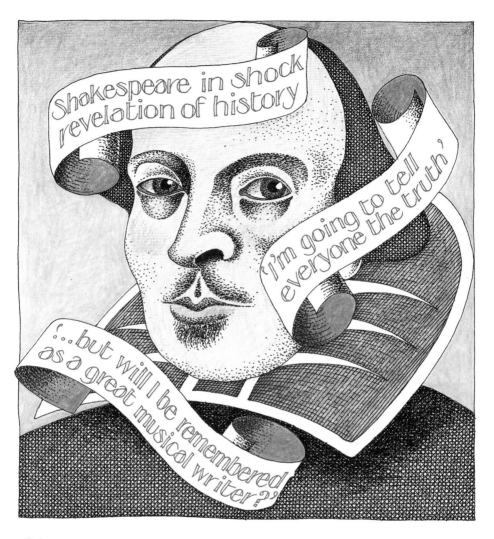

Shakespeare, who scholars revere,
built a theatre and called it the Sphere
but soon changed its name
to The Globe (of great fame)
and his first play was called Mama Mia.

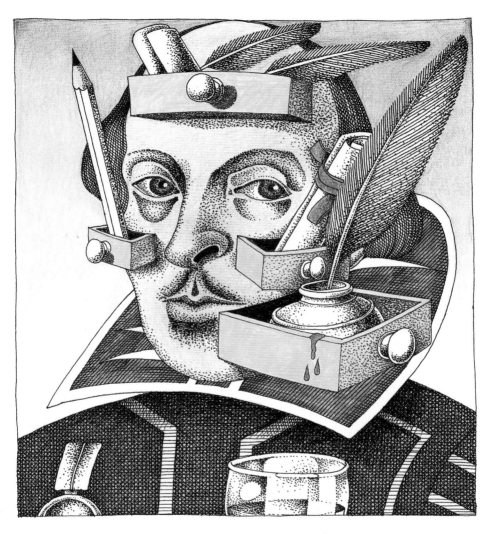

Will Shakespeare was building the Globe
when the monarch awarded an O.B.E.
So with plenty of wine
he penned a first line:
a soliloquy starting with "To be...."

There once was a famous old nurse
who said, whilst observing a hearse,
"When I finish this beer
I'll find the Crimea
and I'll make people better (not worse)."

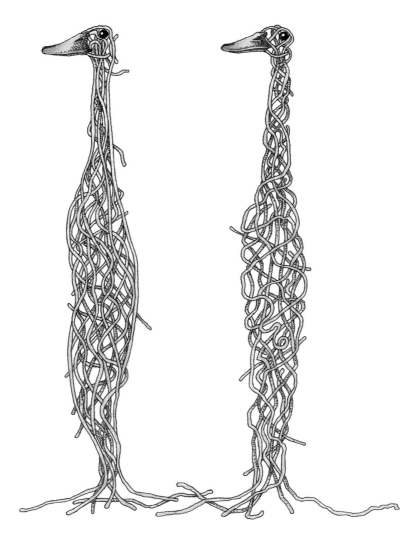

An artist called Gi-a-cometti
made sculptures collected by Getty.
"These figures so thin"
he announced with a grin,
"are made of Italian spaghetti."

There once was a duck who loved cheese.
He believed that it kept off disease.
     "My reasons" he quacked
     "are founded on fact
though I generally do as I please."

A duck with a limp and an egg
was proud of her striped wooden leg
but she hadn't forgotten
the egg had gone rotten
(which explains why she's wearing a peg).

Three shepherds were watching their flock
and hadn't expected the shock:
   an angel appeared
    with a halo and beard.
It was really their dad in a frock.

There were 3. They had gifts. They were wise.
They appeared to have come in disguise.
They kept chewing mints
and dropped a few hints
so we think they were really mint spies.

There was plenty of gossip and banter:
the rumours were all about Santa.
    With several elves
        disgracing themselves
he was found with an empty decanter.

While shopping, Jesus had found
five loaves and two fish for a pound.
That's a pretty good deal
and enough for a meal....
then five thousand neighbours came round.

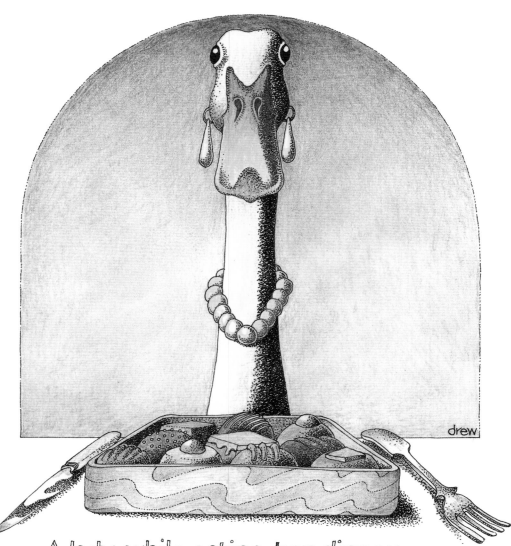

A lady, while eating her dinner,
declared that she'd rather be thinner:
"But food has a race
to get in my face,
and chocolate is always the winner."